Pressure Cooker Miracle Healthy Cookbook

Easy, Inspired Recipes for Eating Well

Terry Mckenzie

Sommario

Introduction..**9**

Lunch **11**

Chicken with Potato plus Rice..................................**11**

Tyrolese Egg Salad..**13**

Asian-Style Savory Egg Custard.............................**15**

Fluffy Scrambled Eggs **17**

Broccoli with Asiago Cheese **19**

Scamorza Open Tart **21**

Savory Muffins with Canadian Bacon **23**

Peppery and Cheesy Deviled Eggs **25**

Three-Cheese and Beer Dip.....................................**27**

Indian Egg Muffins..**29**

Manchego, Sausage and Vegetable Bake 32

Ooey Gooey, Cheesy Pizza 34

Egg Salad with Poppy Seed Dressing 36

Egg Curry in a Hurry 38

Egg Drop Soup with Gorgonzola 40

Kid-Friendly Mini Frittatas 42

Asparagus and Colby Cheese Frittatas 45

Two-Cheese and Mustard Green Dip 47

Portobello Mushrooms Baked Eggs and Cheese 48

Eggs with Peppers in Tomato Sauce 50

Mélange with Spanish Chorizo 52

Ground Meat and Cheese Dip 54

Bacon, Egg, Lettuce Tomato.....................................56

Green Beans with Cheese and Eggs 58

Indian Egg Bhurji 60

Winter Bacon and Leek Quiche 62

Honey Baked Ham 64

Italian-Style Braised Pork Chops 65

Spinach and Feta Stuffed Chicken 68

Pot Roast 70

Shrimp Gumbo 72

Beer Cheese Soup 74

Tahini Lamb Meatballs with Couscous and Pickled Onions 76

Lemon-Herb Chicken 79

BBQ Meatballs 81

Mac Cincinnati Chili..83

Salmon with Spinach and Potatoes.......................86

Pork Tenderloin with Sriracha and Honey...................88

Oregano Scallops Alfredo.......................................90

Burrito Shredded Chicken and Rice Bowl 92

Savory Pie...95

Corned Beef with Cabbage....................................98

Beef and Barley Soup...100

Softly Turkey Breast 102

Pork Meatball with Cream Sauce............................104

Chipotle Brisket 107

Barbecue Spare Ribs..110

Family Pork Roast..112

Conclusion .... Errore. Il segnalibro non è definito.

Introduction

Vegetarianism describes a lifestyle that leaves out the intake of all forms of meat, including pork, poultry, beef, lamb, venison, fish, and coverings.

Depending on a person's beliefs as well as way of life, vegetarianism has different spectrums. There are vegetarians who like to eat items that originate from animals such as milk, eggs, lotion and cheese. At the other end of the range are vegans.

Vegans never consume meat or any kind of products that originate from pets.
The vegan diet regimen has several benefits, actually, the non-meat intake even adhering to the viewpoint of many professionals can likewise be a benefit for our body.
Actually, this type of diet plan is an exceptional method to achieve peace in between your body as well as your mind, always remember not to abandon your principles.

Enjoy analysis our succulent recipes.

Lunch

Chicken with Potato plus Rice

Ingredients for 8 servings: Marinade Ingredients: 1 tablespoon dark soy sauce 1 tablespoon light soy sauce ¼ teaspoon white pepper powder 2 tablespoon Water 1 tablespoon corn starch Other Ingredients: 2 tablespoons olive oil 1 green onion cut in 2-inch length pieces 1 piece Ginger fresh, sliced 1 star anise 3 cloves 400 grams chicken thighs. Boneless and skinless, cut to small pieces 2 cups chicken stock low sodium, or water 1 ½ tablespoons dark soy sauce 1 tablespoon light soy sauce ½ teaspoon salt 1 ⅓ cups white long rice 3 medium yellow potatoes peeled and cut in ¼ inch pieces 1 green onion finely chopped 1 tablespoon sesame oil

Directions and total time – 30-60 m • Mix the chicken meat and all marinade ingredients the night before. Store in a container with a lid and place in the fridge overnight. • Select Sauté, heat olive oil over medium-high heat. • Add in 1 green onion (cut in 2 inches), star anise, fresh ginger, cloves and cook for a minute. • Add the marinated chicken meat, stir frequently for about 3 to 4 minutes until outside of chicken turns light brown, set aside. • Transfer all cooked chicken with liquid into the Instant Pot. Add the chicken broth, dark and light soy sauces, salt, rice, and potatoes. • Close the lid, make sure the valve is set to "Sealing" position. Select the "Rice" function and allow to cook for 12 minutes by adjusting the time. • When time is done, wait for another 10 minutes then quick release the pressure and open the lid. • Stir in finely chopped green onion and sesame oil. Cover the pot with the lid and let the rice sit for 5 minutes before serving.

Tyrolese Egg Salad

(Ready in about 30 minutes | Servings 4)

Per serving: 342 Calories; 29.2g Fat; 7.2g Carbs; 12.7g Protein; 3.6g Sugars

Ingredients 6 eggs 1/2 pound green beans, trimmed 1 cup of water 3 slices prosciutto, chopped 1/2 cup green onions, chopped 1 carrot, shredded 1/2 cup mayonnaise 1 tablespoon apple cider vinegar 1 teaspoon yellow mustard 4 tablespoons Gorgonzola cheese, crumbled

Directions Pour the water into the Instant Pot; add a steamer basket to the bottom. Arrange the eggs in a steamer basket. Secure the lid. Choose "Manual" mode and High pressure; cook for 5 minutes. Once cooking is complete, use a natural pressure release; carefully remove the lid. Allow the eggs to cool for 15 minutes. Peel the eggs and cut them into slices. Then, add green beans and 1 cup of water to your Instant Pot. Secure the lid. Choose "Manual" mode and Low pressure; cook for 5 minutes.

Once cooking is complete, use a quick pressure release; carefully remove the lid. Transfer green beans to a salad bowl. Add prosciutto, green onions, carrot, mayonnaise, vinegar, and mustard. Top with Gorgonzola cheese and sliced eggs. Enjoy!

Asian-Style Savory Egg Custard

(Ready in about 15 minutes | Servings 3)

Per serving: 234 Calories; 16.8g Fat; 3.6g Carbs; 16.4g Protein; 1.8g Sugars

Ingredients

3 eggs, well beaten 1 cup broth, preferably homemade Kosher salt and white pepper, to taste 1 tablespoon tamari sauce 1/2 tablespoon oyster sauce 1/2 cup Comté cheese, grated

Directions

Place the beaten eggs in a mixing bowl. Slowly and gradually, add broth, whisking constantly as you go. Season with salt and paper. Then, pour this mixture through a strainer. Add tamari sauce and oyster sauce. Pour the mixture into three ramekins. Now, cover the ramekins with a piece of foil. Place the ramekins on the metal trivet. Secure the lid. Choose "Manual" mode and Low pressure; cook for 7 minutes. Once cooking is complete, use a natural pressure release; carefully remove the lid. Top with cheese and serve immediately. Bon appétit!

Fluffy Scrambled Eggs

(Ready in about 10 minutes | Servings 2)

Per serving: 322 Calories; 25.6g Fat; 3.1g Carbs; 18.4g Protein; 1.3g Sugars

Ingredients

4 eggs, beaten 2 tablespoons full cream milk 1 tablespoon ghee, melted Salt, to taste 1/4 teaspoon ground black pepper, or more to taste 1/2 teaspoon smoked paprika

Directions

Begin by adding 1 cup of water and a metal rack to the Instant Pot. Spritz a heatproof bowl with a nonstick cooking spray. Mix all ingredients until well combined. Spoon the mixture into the prepared bowl; lower the bowl onto the rack. Secure the lid. Choose "Manual" mode and Low pressure; cook for 6 minutes. Once cooking is complete, use a natural pressure release; carefully remove the lid. Serve with a dollop of sour cream and tomatoes if desired. Bon appétit!

Broccoli with Asiago Cheese

(Ready in about 12 minutes | Servings 4)

Per serving: 160 Calories; 11.7g Fat; 5.3g Carbs; 10.1g Protein; 0.9g Sugars

Ingredients

1 tablespoon olive oil 2 tablespoons green onion, chopped 4 cloves garlic, pressed 1 pound broccoli, broken into florets 1 cup water 2 chicken bouillon cubes Sea salt and ground black pepper, to taste 3/4 cup Asiago cheese, shredded

Directions

Press the "Sauté" button to heat up your Instant Pot. Now, heat the oil and sweat green onions for 2 minutes. Stir in the garlic and continue to sauté an additional 30 seconds. Add broccoli, water, bouillon cubes, salt, and black pepper. Secure the lid. Choose "Manual" mode and High pressure; cook for 7 minutes. Once cooking is complete, use a natural pressure release; carefully remove the lid. Top with shredded cheese and serve immediately.

Bon appétit!

Scamorza Open Tart

(Ready in about 30 minutes | Servings 4)

Per serving: 350 Calories; 25.1g Fat; 4.8g Carbs; 25.9g Protein; 2.9g Sugars

Ingredients

5 eggs, beaten 1/3 cup double cream Salt and ground black pepper, to taste 1 teaspoon cayenne pepper 5 ounces speck, chopped 1/4 cup scallions, chopped 1/2 cup Scamorza cheese, crumbled 1 bunch of Rucola, to serve

Directions

Begin by adding 1 cup of water and a metal rack to your Instant Pot. Then, spritz a heatproof bowl and set aside. In a mixing dish, thoroughly combine the eggs, cream, salt, black pepper, and cayenne pepper. Add chopped speck, scallions, and cheese. Spoon the mixture into the prepared heatproof bowl; cover with a piece of aluminum foil, making a foil sling. Secure the lid. Choose

"Manual" mode and High pressure; cook for 25 minutes. Once cooking is complete, use a quick pressure release; carefully remove the lid. Garnish with Rucola and serve. Bon appétit!

Savory Muffins with Canadian Bacon

(Ready in about 10 minutes | Servings 4)

Per serving: 301 Calories; 41.3g Fat; 7.8g Carbs; 25.5g Protein; 3.5g Sugars

Ingredients

5 ounces Canadian bacon, sliced 1/2 cup Asiago cheese, shredded 4 eggs, beaten 2 tablespoons butter 2 tablespoons double cream Salt and black pepper, to taste 1/2 teaspoon red pepper flakes, crushed 1/2 teaspoon granulated garlic 1/4 cup shallots, minced 2 tablespoons coriander, chopped

Directions

Line muffin cups with bacon slices. Then, add a layer of cheese. In a mixing dish, whisk the eggs, butter, double cream, salt, black pepper, red pepper, and garlic. Pour the egg mixture over cheese. Sprinkle with minced shallots and coriander. Add 1 cup of water and a metal trivet to the Instant Pot. Now, place the muffin cups on the trivet. Secure the lid. Choose "Manual" mode and High pressure; cook for 6 minutes. Once cooking is complete, use a natural pressure release; carefully remove the lid. Allow the muffins to stand for a few minutes before removing from the cups. Bon appétit!

Peppery and Cheesy Deviled Eggs

(Ready in about 25 minutes | Servings 4)

Per serving: 264 Calories; 21.1g Fat; 6g Carbs; 11.7g Protein; 3.8g Sugars

Ingredients

6 eggs 1 teaspoon canola oil 1 onion, chopped 2 bell peppers, drained and chopped Seasoned salt and freshly ground black pepper, to taste 1/4 cup mayonnaise 1 teaspoon mustard 1 tablespoon fresh lemon juice 4 tablespoons Colby cheese, grated 1 teaspoon smoked Hungarian paprika

Directions

Pour the water into the Instant Pot; add a steamer basket to the bottom. Arrange the eggs in a steamer basket if you have one. Secure the lid. Choose "Manual" mode and High pressure; cook for 5 minutes. Once cooking is complete, use a natural pressure release; carefully remove the lid. Allow the eggs to cool for 15 minutes. Peel the eggs and separate egg whites from yolks. Press the "Sauté" button to heat up your Instant Pot; heat the oil. Now, sauté the onion along with peppers until softened. Season with salt and pepper. Add the reserved egg yolks to the pepper mixture. Stir in mayo, mustard, and lemon juice. Now, stuff the egg whites with this mixture. Top with grated Colby cheese and arrange the stuffed eggs on a serving platter. Afterwards, sprinkle Hungarian paprika over eggs and serve.

Three-Cheese and Beer Dip

(Ready in about 10 minutes | Servings 10)

Per serving: 220 Calories; 14.9g Fat; 2.9g Carbs; 18.1g Protein; 1.7g Sugars

Ingredients

16 ounces Cottage cheese, softened 5 ounces goat cheese, softened 1/2 teaspoon garlic powder 1 teaspoon stone-ground mustard 1/2 cup chicken stock, preferably homemade 1/2 cup lager beer 6 ounces pancetta, chopped 1 cup Monterey-Jack cheese, shredded 2 tablespoons fresh chives, roughly chopped

Directions

Add Cottage cheese, goat cheese, garlic powder, mustard, chicken stock, beer, and pancetta to the Instant Pot. Secure the lid. Choose "Manual" mode and High pressure; cook for 4 minutes. Once cooking is complete, use a quick pressure release; carefully remove the lid. Press the "Sauté" button to heat up your Instant

Pot. Add Monterey-Jack cheese and stir until everything is thoroughly warmed. Sprinkle with fresh chopped chives and serve. Bon appétit!

Indian Egg Muffins

(Ready in about 10 minutes | Servings 5)

Per serving: 202 Calories; 13.7g Fat; 4.7g Carbs; 15.4g Protein; 2.6g Sugars

Ingredients

5 eggs Seasoned salt and ground black pepper, to taste 2 green chilies, minced 5 tablespoons feta cheese, crumbled 1/2 tablespoon Chaat masala powder 1 tablespoon fresh cilantro, finely chopped

Directions

Begin by adding 1 cup of water and a steamer basket to your Instant Pot. Mix all ingredients together; then, spoon the egg/cheese mixture into silicone muffin cups. Next, lower your muffin cups onto the steamer basket. Secure the lid. Choose "Manual" mode and High pressure; cook for 7 minutes. Once cooking is complete, use a quick pressure release; carefully remove the lid. Let your muffins sit for a few minutes before removing from the cups; serve warm. Bon appétit!

Manchego, Sausage and Vegetable Bake

(Ready in about 25 minutes | Servings 4)

Per serving: 344 Calories; 27.4g Fat; 3g Carbs; 20.3g Protein; 1.3g Sugars

Ingredients

8 slices pork sausage, chopped 1 ½ cups mushrooms, sliced 1 garlic clove, minced 1 cup kale leaves, torn into pieces 7 eggs 1/3 cup milk 1 cup Manchego cheese, shredded Sea salt and freshly ground black pepper, to taste

Directions

Press the "Sauté" button to heat up the Instant Pot. Now, cook the sausage until no longer pink. Then, add mushrooms and garlic; continue to cook until they are fragrant; turn off the Instant Pot; add kale and let it sit for 5 minutes. Wipe down your Instant Pot with a damp cloth. Add 1 cup of water and a metal rack. Spritz a baking dish that fits into your Instant Pot. In a mixing bowl, thoroughly combine the eggs, milk, cheese, salt and black pepper; add the sausage/vegetable mixture to the mixing bowl. Spoon the mixture into the baking dish. Lower the baking dish onto the rack. Secure the lid. Choose "Manual" mode and High pressure; cook for 15 minutes. Once cooking is complete, use a quick pressure release; carefully remove the lid. Enjoy!

Ooey Gooey, Cheesy Pizza

(Ready in about 20 minutes | Servings 6)

Per serving: 334 Calories; 25.1g Fat; 5.9g Carbs; 20.5g Protein; 2.8g Sugars

Ingredients

1 tablespoon olive oil 1 large-sized tomato, chopped 6 ounces pepperoni 1 yellow onion, chopped 2 bell peppers, chopped 1 cup mozzarella cheese, sliced 1/2 cup provolone cheese, sliced 3 eggs, whisked 1/2 teaspoon dried basil 1/2 teaspoon dried oregano 1/2 teaspoon dried rosemary 1/2 cup Kalamata olives, pitted and halved

Directions

Grease the bottom and sides of your Instant Pot with olive oil. Place 1/2 of chopped tomato on the bottom. Then, layer 3 ounces of pepperoni, 1/2 of yellow onion, 1 bell pepper, 1/2 cup of mozzarella cheese and 1/4 cup of provolone cheese. Continue layering until you run out of ingredients. Pour in the whisked eggs. Afterwards, sprinkle seasonings and olives over the top. Secure the lid. Choose "Manual" mode and High pressure; cook for 15 minutes. Once cooking is complete, use a natural pressure release; carefully remove the lid. Serve warm.

Egg Salad with Poppy Seed Dressing

(Ready in about 25 minutes | Servings 4)

Per serving: 340 Calories; 27.5g Fat; 8.1g Carbs; 16.4g Protein; 2.9g Sugars

Ingredients

5 medium-sized eggs 1/2 pound kale leaves, torn into pieces 1/2 cup radishes, sliced 1 white onion, thinly sliced 2 tablespoons champagne vinegar 1/2 tablespoon poppy seeds Sea salt and white pepper, to taste 1/2 teaspoon cayenne pepper 1 teaspoon yellow mustard 1/4 cup extra-virgin olive oil 3 ounces goat cheese, crumbled

Directions

Pour 1 cup of water into the Instant Pot; add a steamer basket to the bottom. Arrange the eggs in the steamer basket. Secure the lid. Choose "Manual" mode and High pressure; cook for 5 minutes. Once cooking is complete, use a natural pressure release; carefully remove the lid. Allow the eggs to cool for 15 minutes. Then, place them in your refrigerator and reserve. Then, place kale in the steamer basket. Secure the lid. Choose "Manual" mode and High pressure; cook for 1 minute. Once cooking is complete, use a quick pressure release; carefully remove the lid. Now, place radishes and onion in a salad bowl. Add kale and sliced eggs. In a mixing dish, thoroughly combine vinegar, poppy seeds, salt, white pepper, cayenne pepper, and olive oil. Pour the dressing over your salad. Top with goat cheese and serve well-chilled. Bon appétit!

Egg Curry in a Hurry

(Ready in about 20 minutes | Servings 6)

Per serving: 253 Calories; 19.7g Fat; 4.9g Carbs; 13.9g Protein; 2.5g Sugars

Ingredients

1 ½ tablespoons butter, melted 1 yellow onion, chopped 1 ½ tablespoons curry paste 2 ripe tomatoes, peeled and chopped 1 cup water 7 eggs, whisked 1/2 cup cheddar cheese, grated

Directions

Press the "Sauté" button to heat up the Instant Pot. Now, warm the butter; once hot, sauté the onion until softened and fragrant. Add the remaining ingredients and stir to combine. Secure the lid. Choose "Manual" mode and High pressure; cook for 10 minutes. Once cooking is complete, use a quick pressure release; carefully remove the lid. Enjoy!

Egg Drop Soup with Gorgonzola

(Ready in about 20 minutes | Servings 4

Per serving: 163 Calories; 11.7g Fat; 3.1g Carbs; 10.8g Protein; 1.1g Sugars

Ingredients

1 tablespoon olive oil 1 carrot, chopped 1 clove garlic, minced 3 cups beef bone broth 1/2 cup water 2 eggs, slightly whisked Sea salt and ground black pepper, to your liking 1 teaspoon celery seeds 1/2 teaspoon paprika 1/2 cup Gorgonzola cheese, crumbled 1 heaping tablespoon fresh chives, minced

Directions

Press the "Sauté" button to heat up the Instant Pot. Now, heat the olive oil and cook the carrot and garlic until fragrant. Add broth and water. Secure the lid. Choose "Manual" mode and High pressure; cook for 10 minutes. Once cooking is complete, use a quick pressure release; carefully remove the lid. Then, mix the eggs, salt, black pepper, celery seeds, paprika, and cheese until well blended. Stir this mixture into the Instant Pot and press the "Sauté" button. Whisk until heated through. Serve in individual bowls, garnished with fresh chives. Enjoy!

Kid-Friendly Mini Frittatas

(Ready in about 15 minutes | Servings 4)

Per serving: 314 Calories; 25.6g Fat; 2.9g Carbs; 16.7g Protein; 1.7g Sugars

Ingredients

4 eggs 1/4 cup full-fat milk Sea salt, to taste 1/4 teaspoon ground black pepper 1/4 teaspoon cayenne pepper, or more to taste 1/2 teaspoon granulated garlic 1/3 teaspoon ground bay leaf 1/2 teaspoon dried dill weed 1 cup Chorizo sausage, chopped 1/2 cup green onions, chopped

Directions

Prepare your Instant Pot by adding 1 cup of water and a metal trivet to the bottom of the inner pot. Thoroughly combine all ingredients until everything is well mixed. Spoon the mixture into silicone molds. Lower the silicone molds onto the trivet. Secure the lid. Choose "Manual" mode and High pressure; cook for 7 minutes.

Once cooking is complete, use a quick pressure release; carefully remove the lid. Bon appétit!

_____

Asparagus and Colby Cheese Frittatas

(Ready in about 25 minutes | Servings 6

Per serving: 272 Calories; 21.1g Fat; 4.7g Carbs; 15.5g Protein; 2.3g Sugars

Ingredients

1 tablespoon butter, softened 1/2 cup leeks, chopped 2 garlic cloves, minced 10 asparagus spears, chopped 6 eggs, beaten 4 tablespoons milk 3 tablespoons cream cheese Kosher salt and white pepper, to taste 1/2 teaspoon thyme, minced 1/2 teaspoon rosemary, minced 1 cup Colby cheese, shredded

Directions

Press the "Sauté" button to heat up the Instant Pot. Now, melt the butter and sauté the leeks until softened. Add garlic and cook an additional 30 seconds. Turn off your Instant Pot. Add the remaining ingredients and mix to combine. Spoon the mixture into lightly greased ramekins. Wipe down your Instant Pot with a damp cloth.

Place 1 cup of water and a rack in your Instant Pot. Lower the ramekins onto the rack. Cover them with a piece of foil. Secure the lid. Choose "Soup/Broth" mode and Low pressure; cook for 20 minutes. Once cooking is complete, use a quick pressure release; carefully remove the lid. Bon appétit!

Two-Cheese and Mustard Green Dip

(Ready in about 10 minutes | Servings 8)

Per serving: 49 Calories; 3.1g Fat; 1.4g Carbs; 3.9g Protein; 0.8g Sugars

Ingredients

1 cup mustard greens, chopped 4 ounces Cottage cheese, at room temperature 1/2 cup goat cheese, at room temperature Salt and ground black pepper, to taste 1 teaspoon Dijon mustard

Directions

Simply throw all of the above ingredients into your Instant Pot. Secure the lid. Choose "Manual" mode and Low pressure; cook for 3 minutes. Once cooking is complete, use a quick pressure release; carefully remove the lid. Serve warm and enjoy!

Portobello Mushrooms Baked Eggs and Cheese

(Ready in about 10 minutes | Servings 4)

Per serving: 256 Calories; 18.6g Fat; 5.3g Carbs; 17g Protein; 2.9g Sugars

Ingredients

4 medium-sized Portobello mushrooms, stems removed 4 eggs 1 red bell pepper, deveined and chopped 1 green bell pepper, deveined and chopped Sea salt and ground black pepper, to your liking 1/2 teaspoon cayenne pepper 1/2 teaspoon dried dill weed 1 cup Pepper-Jack cheese, grated

Directions

Start by adding 1 cup of water and a metal trivet to your Instant Pot. Spritz Portobello mushrooms with a nonstick cooking spray. Mix the eggs, pepper, salt, black pepper, cayenne pepper, and dill; mix until everything is well combined. Spoon this mixture into the prepared mushrooms caps. Place the stuffed mushrooms onto the metal trivet. Secure the lid. Choose "Manual" mode and High pressure; cook for 6 minutes. Once cooking is complete, use a quick pressure release; carefully remove the lid. Top with shredded cheese. Bon appétit!

Eggs with Peppers in Tomato Sauce

(Ready in about 10 minutes | Servings 4)

Per serving: 171 Calories; 12.2g Fat; 7.6g Carbs; 8.4g Protein; 4.1g Sugars

Ingredients

2 tablespoons olive oil 1 shallot, diced 1 teaspoon garlic paste 2 bell peppers, diced Salt and freshly ground black pepper, to taste 1 teaspoon cayenne pepper 1 teaspoon dried basil 2 ripe tomatoes, puréed 5 eggs 2 heaping tablespoons chives, chopped

Directions

Press the "Sauté" button to heat up your Instant Pot. Now, heat the olive oil and sauté the shallot until tender and aromatic. Add the garlic paste, peppers, salt, black pepper, cayenne pepper, basil, and tomatoes. Then, crack the eggs into the vegetable mixture. Secure the lid. Choose "Manual" mode and Low pressure; cook for 5 minutes. Once cooking is complete, use a quick pressure release; carefully remove the lid. Serve garnished with chopped chives. Enjoy!

Mélange with Spanish Chorizo

(Ready in about 25 minutes | Servings 6)

Per serving: 385 Calories; 30.2g Fat; 6.5g Carbs; 21.2g Protein; 3.1g Sugars

Ingredients

8 eggs 2 tablespoons olive oil 1/2 cup leeks, chopped 1 carrot, chopped 1 teaspoon fresh garlic, minced 1/2 cup Spanish chorizo, finely diced 2 ripe Roma tomatoes, puréed 2 sprigs fresh thyme 2 sprigs fresh rosemary 1 bay leaf Sea salt and ground black pepper, to taste 1/2 teaspoon smoked paprika 1 cup chicken stock 1 cup white cheddar cheese, shredded

Directions

Place 1 cup of water and a steamer basket in your Instant Pot. Now, arrange the eggs on the steamer basket. Secure the lid. Choose "Manual" mode and Low pressure; cook for 5 minutes. Once cooking is complete, use a quick pressure release; carefully remove the lid. Allow the eggs to cool and then, chop them roughly. Press the "Sauté" button to heat up your Instant Pot. Now, heat the olive oil until sizzling. Once hot, cook the leeks until they are softened. Add the carrot, garlic and chorizo; cook an additional minute or until just softened. Add tomatoes, thyme, rosemary, bay leaf, salt, pepper, paprika, and stock. Add the reserved hard-boiled eggs. Secure the lid. Choose "Manual" mode and High pressure; cook for 10 minutes. Once cooking is complete, use a quick pressure release; carefully remove the lid. Top with cheddar cheese, cover with the lid and let it sit until the cheese is completely melted. Bon appétit!

Ground Meat and Cheese Dip

(Ready in about 10 minutes | Servings 10

Per serving: 254 Calories; 17.9g Fat; 3.9g Carbs; 18.8g Protein; 2.6g Sugars

Ingredients

2 teaspoons olive oil 1 yellow onion, chopped 1/2 pound ground pork 1/2 pound ground beef 1 teaspoon chili powder Sea salt, to taste 1/3 teaspoon freshly ground black pepper 1 tomato, chopped 1/3 cup salsa verde 1/2 cup chicken stock 7 ounces Mascarpone cheese, room temperature 5 ounces Colby cheese, grated

Directions

Press the "Sauté" button to heat up your Instant Pot. Now, heat the oil and cook the onion until tender. Next, cook the pork and beef until no longer pink, about 4 minutes. After that, add chili powder, salt, black pepper, tomato, and salsa verde. Secure the lid. Choose "Manual" mode and High pressure; cook for 5 minutes. Once cooking is complete, use a natural pressure release; carefully remove the lid. Add cheese and cover with the lid. Let it sit in the residual heat until everything is well combined. Enjoy!

Bacon, Egg, Lettuce Tomato

(Ready in about 10 minutes | Servings 4)

Per serving: 258 Calories; 20.1g Fat; 5.5g Carbs; 14.1g Protein; 3.1g Sugars

Ingredients

4 eggs Salt and freshly ground black pepper, to taste 4 slices bacon 8 leaves lettuce 1 large-sized tomato, sliced

Directions

Add 1 cup of water and a metal trivet to the Instant Pot. Spritz four silicone cups with a nonstick cooking spray. Crack an egg into each cup. Then, lower the silicone cups onto the metal trivet. Secure the lid. Choose "Steam" mode and High pressure; cook for 4 minutes. Once cooking is complete, use a quick pressure release; carefully remove the lid. Season your eggs with salt and pepper. Press the "Sauté" button to heat up your Instant Pot. Once hot, cook the bacon until crisp and browned. Divide lettuce leaves between four serving plates. Add bacon slice on each serving; place a few slices of tomato on each serving. Top with poached eggs and serve warm. Bon appétit!

Green Beans with Cheese and Eggs

(Ready in about 10 minutes | Servings 4)

Per serving: 249 Calories; 19.4g Fat; 7.2g Carbs; 12.2g Protein; 2.6g Sugars

Ingredients

2 tablespoons olive oil 2 garlic cloves, pressed 1 pound green beans, sliced 4 eggs, slightly whisked Salt and freshly ground black pepper, to taste 1 cup stock, preferably homemade 1 cup feta cheese, crumbled

Directions

Press the "Sauté" button to heat up your Instant Pot. Now, heat the olive oil until sizzling. Once hot, stir in garlic and cook for 40 seconds or until fragrant. Add green beans, eggs, salt, pepper, and stock. Secure the lid. Choose "Manual" mode and Low pressure; cook for 3 minutes. Once cooking is complete, use a quick pressure release; carefully remove the lid. Afterwards, add feta cheese and serve immediately.

Indian Egg Bhurji

(Ready in about 15 minutes | Servings 4

Per serving: 259 Calories; 20.6g Fat; 4.6g Carbs; 13.4g Protein; 2.6g Sugars

Ingredients

1 ½ tablespoons sesame oil 1/2 yellow onion, chopped 2 garlic cloves, minced 1 (1/2-inch) piece fresh ginger, grated 2 cups Cremini mushrooms, sliced 4 eggs, beaten 4 tablespoons full-fat milk Table salt and ground black pepper, to taste 1/4 teaspoon turmeric 1 teaspoon garam masala 1/2 cup Pepper-Jack cheese, preferably freshly grated

Directions

Press the "Sauté" button to heat up your Instant Pot. Heat the oil and cook the onion until they are caramelized; add a splash of water if needed. After that, stir in the garlic, ginger, and mushrooms; continue to cook an additional 1 minute or until fragrant. Add beaten eggs, milk, salt, pepper, turmeric, and garam masala. Secure the lid. Choose "Manual" mode and High pressure; cook for 7 minutes. Once cooking is complete, use a quick pressure release; carefully remove the lid. Add Pepper-Jack cheese and put the lid on the Instant Pot. Let it sit in the residual heat for 3 to 5 minutes. Serve warm and enjoy!

Winter Bacon and Leek Quiche

(Ready in about 35 minutes | Servings 6)

Per serving: 231 Calories; 15.2g Fat; 6.9g Carbs; 16.5g Protein; 3.1g Sugars

Ingredients

4 slices Canadian bacon, chopped 1 cup leeks, chopped 1 garlic clove, minced 8 eggs 1/2 cup half-and-half 1/2 cup cream cheese, room temperature Seasoned salt and ground black pepper, to taste 1 tablespoon dried sage, crushed 1/2 teaspoon marjoram 1/2 cup Swiss cheese, freshly grated

Directions

Press the "Sauté" button to heat up your Instant Pot. Once hot, cook the bacon until crisp and browned. Add the leeks and garlic and cook 1 minute more. Add the eggs, half-and-half, cream cheese, salt, black pepper, sage and marjoram. Grease a baking pan with a nonstick cooking spray. Spoon the bacon/egg mixture into the prepared baking pan. Now, add 1 cup of water and a metal trivet to the Instant Pot; lower the baking pan onto the trivet. Secure the lid. Choose "Meat/Stew" mode and High pressure; cook for 25 minutes. Once cooking is complete, use a quick pressure release; carefully remove the lid. Add Swiss cheese and cover with the lid; let it sit in the residual heat for 5 minutes. Serve with Dijon mustard.

Honey Baked Ham

Ingredients for 6-8 servings:

Glaze: 4 garlic cloves minced 4 tbs orange marmalade/jam 4 tbs Dijon mustard 3 tbs brown sugar 1 orange zested 1 cup Freshly Squeezed Orange Juice 1 tbs fresh rosemary Ham: 2 lb fully cooked smoked ham

Directions and total time – 30-60 m

• In a small bowl mix the garlic, orange marmalade (or jam), Dijon mustard, brown sugar, orange zest and orange juice. Use a hand blender to blend all the ingredients until you get a smooth glaze. Add the fresh thyme to the mixture. • Set your Instant Poti oven on Bake function at 360°F for 50 minutes. Place the ham on top of the baking pan and pour the glaze over the ham. • The ham is done when it is heated (the internal temperature should be ~145°F), and the glaze develops a golden-brown color.

Italian-Style Braised Pork Chops

Ingredients for 4 servings:

1 cup chicken broth 2 tbsp balsamic vinegar 2 tsp stemmed thyme leaves or 1 tsp dried thyme ¼ tsp grated fresh nutmeg or ⅛ tsp ground nutmeg ¼ tsp red pepper flakes ¼ tsp table salt 4 cups frozen bell pepper strips 16-ounce bag 4 frozen center-cut boneless pork loin chops 6-8-ounce each

Directions and total time – 30 m

• Stir the broth, vinegar, thyme, nutmeg, red pepper flakes, and salt in an Instant Pot. Mix in the frozen pepper strips, then set the pork chops in the pot so they stand up on their sides and lean against each other and the side of the insert with room between each for liquid and pepper strips (in other words, not in a stack). Lock the lid onto the pot. • Option 1 Max Pressure Cooker • Press Pressure cook on Max pressure for 16 minutes with the Keep Warm setting off. • Optional 2 All Pressure Cookers • Press Meat/Stew, Pressure Cook or Manual on High pressure for 20 minutes with the Keep Warm setting off. The vent must be closed. • Use the quick-release method to bring the pot's pressure back to normal. Unlatch the lid and open the cooker. Transfer the pork chops to serving plates and spoon some of the sauce and peppers over each.

Spinach and Feta Stuffed Chicken

Ingredients for 4 servings:

4 boneless, skinless chicken breasts butterflied (6 ounce ½ cup frozen spinach ⅓ cup crumbled feta cheese 1 ¼ tsp salt divided ¼ tsp pepper ¼ tsp garlic powder ¼ tsp dried oregano ¼ tsp dried parsley 2 tbsp coconut oil 1 cup Water

Directions and total time – 20 m2

• Pound chicken breasts to ¼-inch thickness. In medium bowl, mix frozen spinach and feta and add ¼ teaspoon salt. Evenly divide mixture and spoon onto chicken breasts. • Close chicken breasts and secure with toothpicks or butcher's string. Sprinkle remaining seasonings onto chicken. Press the Sauté button and add coconut oil to Instant Pot. Sear each chicken breast until golden brown (this may take two batches). Press the Cancel button. • Remove chicken and set aside briefly. Pour water into Instant Pot and scrape bottom to remove any chicken or seasoning that is stuck on. Place steam rack into pot. • Place chicken on steam rack and click lid closed. Press 'Pressure Cook' and adjust time for 15 minutes. When timer beeps, allow a 15-minute natural release, then quick-release the remaining pressure. Serve warm with favorite white sauce if desired.

Pot Roast

Ingredients for 6 servings:

2 ½ lbs boneless beef chuck roast (up to 3 lbs 1 tbsp vegetable oil ½ cup dry red wine 2 large Onions cut into large chunks or wedges (about 3 cups) 5 large carrots peeled and cut into 2 inchpieces or2 ½ cups of baby cut carrots 1 lbs whole baby red potatoes or medium red potatoes cut in half 2 sprigs fresh thyme leaves 1 can Condensed Cream of Mushroom Soup 10 ½ ounces

Directions and total time – 1-2 h

• Cut the beef in half crosswise (for quicker cooking), then season with salt and pepper. On a 6 quart Instant Pot, select the Saute setting. Heat the oil. Add the beef (in batches, if needed) and cook for 15 minutes or until well browned on all sides. Remove the beef from the pot. Add the wine and cook, stirring to scrape up the browned bits from the bottom of the pot. Press Cancel. • Layer the onions, carrots, potatoes, thyme and beef in the Instant Pot. Spoon the soup over the beef (the order is important, so don't stir until after the cooking is done). • Lock the lid and close the pressure release valve. Pressure cook on High pressure, setting the timer to 45 minutes (timer will begin counting down once pressure is reachedit takes about 10 minutes). When done, press Cancel and use the quick release method to release the pressure. • Remove the beef to a serving plate, cover and keep warm. Select the Saute setting and cook the vegetables and gravy for 10 minutes or until the gravy is slightly thickened. Remove and discard the thyme. Season to taste. Slice the beef and serve with the vegetables and gravy.

Shrimp Gumbo

Ingredients for 6 servings:

¼ cup vegetable oil ¼ cup all-purpose flour 4 stalks celery chopped 1 large yellow onion peeled and diced 1 large green bell pepper seeded and diced 2 garlic cloves peeled and minced 1 can diced tomatoes 14.5 ounce ¼ tsp dried thyme ¼ tsp cayenne pepper 2 bay leaves 1 tbsp filé powder 2 tsp Worcestershire sauce 4 cups Seafood Stock 1 lb smoked sausage sliced 1 lb medium shrimp peeled and deveined ¼ tsp salt ¼ tsp ground black pepper 2 cups cooked long-grain rice

Directions and total time – 30-60 m

• Press the Sauté button on the Instant Pot and heat oil. Add flour and cook, stirring constantly, until flour is medium brown in color, about 15 minutes. • Add celery, onion, green pepper, garlic, and tomatoes and cook, stirring constantly, until the vegetables are tender, about 8 minutes. Add thyme, cayenne, bay leaves, filé, Worcestershire sauce, and stock and stir well, making sure nothing is stuck to the bottom of the pot, then add sausage. Press the Cancel button. • Close lid and set steam release to Sealing, then press the Manual button and adjust cook time to 8 minutes. When the timer beeps, quick release the pressure. Open lid and stir in shrimp, salt, and black pepper. Press the Cancel button, then press the Sauté button and cook for 8 minutes, or until shrimp are cooked through. Discard bay leaves. Serve hot over rice.

Beer Cheese Soup

Ingredients for 8 servings:

3 tbsp unsalted butter 2 medium carrots peeled and chopped 2 stalks celery chopped 1 medium onion peeled and chopped 1 clove garlic peeled and minced 1 tsp dried mustard ½ tsp smoked paprika ¼ cup all-purpose flour 1 bottle lager beer or ale 12-ounce 4 cups chicken broth ½ cup heavy cream 2 cups shredded sharp cheddar cheese 1 cup shredded smoked Gouda cheese

Directions and total time – 30-60 m

• Press the Sauté button on the Instant Pot and melt butter. Add carrots, celery, and onion. Cook, stirring often, until softened, about 5 minutes. Add garlic and cook until fragrant, about 30 seconds, then add mustard and paprika and stir well. • Add flour and stir well to combine, then cook for 1 minute. Slowly stir in beer, scraping the bottom of pot well, then add broth. Press the Cancel button. • Close lid, set steam release to Sealing, press the Manual button, and set time to 5 minutes. When the timer beeps, let pressure release naturally, about 15 minutes. Open lid and purée mixture with an immersion blender. Stir in cream, then stir in cheese 1 cup

---

Tahini Lamb Meatballs with Couscous and Pickled Onions

Ingredients for 4 servings:

Lamb Meatballs and Couscous Ingredients: ½ cup Tahini Sauce divided 3 tbsp panko bread crumbs 1 lb ground lamb ¼ cup chopped fresh mint divided 1 tsp ground cinnamon divided 1 tsp ground cumin divided ¾ tsp table salt divided 1 tbsp extra-virgin olive oil 1 onion chopped fine ⅛ tsp cayenne pepper 1 cup chicken broth plus extra as needed 1 cup couscous ½ cup jarred roasted red peppers rinsed, patted dry, and chopped 1 tbsp teaspoon grated lemon zest plus 1juice ⅓ cup Quick Pickled Onions Tahini Sauce Ingredients: ½ cup tahini ½ cup Water ¼ cup lemon juice (2 lemons) 2 garlic cloves minced Quick Pickled Onions Ingredients: 1 cup red wine vinegar ⅓ cup sugar ⅛ tsp table salt 1 red onion halved and sliced thin through root end

Directions and total time – 1-2 h

Tahini Sauce Instructions • Whisk all Tahini sauce ingredients in bowl until smooth (mixture will appear broken at first). Season with salt and pepper to taste.

Let sit at room temperature for at least 30 minutes to allow flavors to meld. (Sauce can be refrigerated for up to 4 days; bring to room temperature before serving.) Quick Pickled Onions Instructions • Microwave vinegar, sugar, and salt in medium bowl until simmering, 1 to 2 minutes. Add onion and let sit, stirring occasionally, for 45 minutes. Drain onion and return to now-empty bowl. (Drained onions can be refrigerated for up to 1 week.) Lamb Meatballs and Couscous • Using fork, mash ¼ cup Tahini Sauce and panko together in bowl to form paste. Add ground lamb, 2 tablespoons mint, ½ teaspoon cinnamon, ½ teaspoon cumin, and ½ teaspoon salt, and knead with hands until thoroughly combined. Pinch off and roll mixture into twelve 1 ½ inch meatballs. • Using highest Sauté function, heat oil in Instant Pot until shimmering. Add onion and remaining ¼ teaspoon salt and cook until onion is softened, about 5 minutes. Stir in remaining ½ teaspoon cinnamon, remaining ½ teaspoon cumin, and cayenne and cook until fragrant, about 30 seconds. Stir in broth, scraping up any browned bits. Add meatballs to pot. Lock lid in place and close pressure release valve. Select Pressure Cook function and cook for

1 minute. • Turn off Instant Pot and quick-release pressure. Carefully remove lid, allowing steam to escape away from you. Using slotted spoon, transfer meatballs to plate, tent with aluminum foil, and let rest while cooking couscous. (You should have about 2 cups cooking liquid remaining in pot; add extra broth as needed to equal 2 cups.) • Using highest Sauté function, bring liquid in pot to simmer. Stir in couscous, red peppers, and lemon zest and juice. Turn off Instant Pot, cover, and let sit for 10 minutes. Fluff couscous gently with fork and transfer to serving dish. Arrange meatballs on top and drizzle with remaining ¼ cup Tahini Sauce. Sprinkle with pickled onions and remaining 2 tablespoons mint. Serve.

Lemon-Herb Chicken

Ingredients for 4 servings:

1 Tbsp. oil 1 ½ lbs boneless, skinless chicken breasts cut into strips ½ cup Water 1 jar INSTANT POT Zesty Lemon Herb Sauce 15 oz

Directions and total time – 30-60 m • HEAT oil in Instant Pot using SAUTÉ setting on high heat. Add chicken; cook 5 min., stirring frequently. • ADD water and sauce. Do not stir. Close and lock lid. Turn Pressure Release Valve to Sealing position. • COOK 6 min. using HIGH PRESSURE COOK/MANUAL setting. When timer goes off, use Quick Pressure Release to release pressure before carefully opening lid.

BBQ Meatballs

Ingredients for 40 meatballs:

2 lbs lean ground beef ½ cup finely chopped onions ¼ cup finely chopped fresh parsley 1 tbsp minced Garlic 2 tsp LEA & PERRINS Worcestershire Sauce 1 tsp salt ½ tsp black pepper 2 eggs beaten 1 cup dry bread crumbs divided 1 jar INSTANT POT Southern BBQ Sauce divided, 15 oz ½ cup fat-free reduced-sodium beef broth

Directions and total time – 30-60 m • 1 cup water to INSTANT POT. Place trivet in pot. • Mix first 8 ingredients in large bowl just until blended. Add half the bread crumbs and 2 tbsp barbecue sauce; mix lightly. Gently mix in remaining bread crumbs. • Shape meat mixture into 40 meatballs (½ inch- 1 inch) • Place half the meatballs in single layer on trivet; cover with second layer of meatballs. Close and lock lid. Turn Pressure Release Valve to Sealing position. • Cook 7 min using MANUAL/HIGH PRESSURE COOK setting. When timer goes off, use Natural Pressure Release

for 5 min., then do a Quick Pressure Release to release any remaining steam. Remove lid. • Use tongs to transfer meatballs to serving bowl; cover to keep warm. Remove trivet from INSTANT POT. Discard meat juices from pot. Rinse liner, then return liner to pot. • Add beef broth and remaining barbecue sauce to pot; stir. Cook using SAUTÉ setting 3 min. or until heated through, stirring frequently. Pour over meatballs; stir to evenly coat meatballs with sauce.

Mac Cincinnati Chili

Ingredients for 4 servings:

Spice Blend: 1 tbsp sweet paprika 2 tsp ground cumin 1 ½ tsp ground cinnamon 1 tsp ground coriander 1 tsp natural cocoa powder 1 tsp mustard powder ½ tsp ground ginger ¼ tsp ground cloves ¼ tsp cayenne pepper Other Ingredients: 2 tsp cold-pressed avocado oil 2 garlic cloves minced 1 yellow onion diced, plus ¾ cup chopped, for serving 1 lb 96 percent extra-lean ground beef 2 cups low-sodium roasted beef bone broth 8 oz whole-wheat elbow pasta 14 ½ oz petite diced tomatoes and their liquid one can 1 ½ cups drained cooked kidney beans or 15 oz (1 can) kidney beans, rinsed and drained ¾ cup shredded Cheddar cheese or vegan cheese shreds, for serving yellow mustard for serving Tabasco sauce for serving

Directions and total time – 30-60 m

• To make the spice blend: In a small bowl, stir together the paprika, cumin, cinnamon, coriander, cocoa powder, mustard powder, ginger, cloves, and cayenne. • Select the Sauté setting on the Instant Pot and heat the oil and garlic for 2 minutes, until the garlic is bubbling but not browned. Add the diced onion and sauté. for about 2 minutes, until it begins to soften. Add the beef and sauté. for 3 minutes, using a wooden spoon to break up the meat as it cooks. Stir in the spice blend and sauté. for about 2 more minutes, until the beef is mostly cooked through and the spices are aromatic. • Pour in the broth, using a wooden spoon or spatula to nudge any browned bits from the bottom of the pot. Add the pasta in an even layer, using the spoon to nudge the noodles under the liquid as much as possible. It's fine if a few pieces are sticking up out of the water. Pour the tomatoes and their liquid and the kidney beans evenly over the ground beef and pasta mixture. Do not stir them in. • Secure the lid and set the Pressure Release to Sealing. Press the Cancel button to reset the cooking program, then select the Pressure Cook or Manual setting and set the cooking time for 6 minutes at high pressure. (The pot will take about 10 minutes to come up to pressure before the cooking program begins.) • When the cooking program ends, let the pressure release naturally for 5 minutes, then move the Pressure Release to Venting to release any remaining steam. Open the pot and stir the chili mac to combine. Let sit for 5 minutes, then stir once more.

Salmon with Spinach and Potatoes

Ingredients for 4 servings:

1 lb small red potatoes quartered 1 cup Water 1 ¼ tsp salt divided ¾ tsp black pepper divided 4 salmon filets 5-ounces each ¼ tsp sweet paprika ½ tsp lemon zest 4 garlic cloves minced 2 tbsp avocado oil 4 cups packed baby spinach 4 lemon wedges

Directions and total time – 15-30 m

• Place the potatoes in the inner pot and add 1 cup water, ¼ teaspoon salt, and ¼ teaspoon pepper. Place a steam rack on top of the potatoes. • On top of the salmon add the paprika, lemon zest, ½ teaspoon salt, and ¼ teaspoon pepper and place the salmon on top of the steam rack. Secure the lid. • Press the Manual or Pressure Cook button and adjust the time to 3 minutes. • When the timer beeps, let pressure release naturally until float valve drops and then unlock lid. • Remove the salmon and steam rack from the pot and set aside. • Press the Sauté button and cook the potatoes 1 minute. Add the garlic and cook an additional 2 minutes, stirring frequently. Stir in the oil and the remaining salt and pepper. Use a fork to gently mash the potatoes to achieve a chunky texture. Press the Cancel button. • Add the spinach and stir until wilted, about 1–2 minutes. Serve the salmon and potato and spinach mixture with the lemon wedges.

Pork Tenderloin with Sriracha and Honey

Ingredients for 2-4 servings:

1 lb pork tenderloin (or can use up to 1 ½ lbs) 2 tbsp honey 2 tbsp sriracha hot sauce or to taste 1 ½ tsp kosher salt

Directions and total time – 30-60 m

• Insert the spit through the center of the pork tenderloin. Use a pointed metal skewer to make an initial hole if needed. Thread the rotisserie forks from each side and tighten the screws to hold the pork firmly in place. • In a small bowl, combine the honey, sriracha and salt. Brush evenly over the pork tenderloin. • Place the drip pan in the bottom of the cooking chamber. Using the display panel, select AIRFRY, then adjust the temperature to 350°F and the time to 20 minutes, then touch START. • When the display indicates "Add Food" use the rotisserie fetch tool to lift the spit into the cooking chamber, using the red rotisserie release lever to secure the ends of the spit. Close the door and touch ROTATE.

Oregano Scallops Alfredo

Ingredients for 4 servings:

1 ¾ cups alfredo sauce 16 ouncejar 2 ½ cups chicken or vegetable broth ½ tsp dried oregano ½ tsp garlic powder ½ tsp red pepper flakes 12 oz regular no-yolk, or gluten-free dried egg noodles 1 lb frozen bay scallops

Directions and total time – 30-60 m • Put 1 ½ cups of the alfredo sauce in an Instant Pot. Stir in the broth, oregano, garlic powder, and red pepper flakes until smooth. Stir in the noodles, then set the block of frozen scallops right on top. Lock the lid onto the pot. • Option 1 Max Pressure Cooker Press Pressure cook on Max pressure for 3 minutes with the Keep Warm setting off. • Option 2 All Pressure Cookers Press Meat/Stew or Pressure cook (Manual) on High pressure for 4 minutes with the Keep Warm setting off. • When the machine has finished cooking, turn it off and let its pressure return to normal naturally for 1 minute. Then use the quick-release method to get rid of any residual pressure in the pot. • Unlatch the lid and open the cooker. Stir in the remaining ¼ cup alfredo sauce. Set the lid askew over the pot and let sit for a couple of minutes so the noodles continue to absorb some of the liquid. Serve hot.

Burrito Shredded Chicken and Rice Bowl

Ingredients for 6 servings:

2 tbsp extra-virgin olive oil 2 lbs boneless, skinless chicken breasts 5 - 6 chicken breasts 1 tsp ground cumin ¼ tsp cayenne pepper or taco seasoning 1 medium red or white onion chopped 4 oz green chiles chopped or diced 1 can 1 ½ cups low-sodium chicken broth 15 oz pinto beans drained and rinsed 1 can 3 cups cooked brown rice 2 medium avocados pitted and sliced, for garnish fresh chopped cilantro for garnish Sliced jalapeño for garnish prepared salsa for garnish (optional)

Directions and total time – 30-60 m • Select Sauté and add the olive oil to the inner pot. Once the oil is hot, place the chicken breasts in the pot and brown them for 2 minutes per side. • Press Cancel and add the cumin, cayenne pepper, onion, green chiles, and chicken broth. Using a wooden spoon, scrape up any browned bits stuck to the bottom of the pot. • Lock the lid into place. Select Pressure Cook or Manual; set the pressure to High and the time to 15 minutes. Make sure the steam release knob is in the sealed position. After cooking, naturally release the

pressure for 10 minutes, then quick release any remaining pressure. • Unlock and remove the lid. Use a slotted spoon to transfer the chicken to a cutting board. Shred the chicken using two forks, and then add it back to the pot. Add the pinto beans and stir the ingredients to combine. • Serve immediately, or place the chicken and rice in an airtight container and refrigerate for up to 4 days or freeze for up to 2 months. • When ready to serve, divide the rice among six bowls and ladle the chicken mixture on top. Garnish each bowl with 2 slices of fresh avocado, cilantro, jalapeño, and a spoonful of salsa (if using).

Savory Pie

Ingredients for 4-6 servings:

Beef Mixture: 1 lb ground beef preferably 93% lean 1 onion finely diced 1 ½ cups frozen peas and carrots mixture 1 cup mushrooms roughly chopped 2 tbsp Worcestershire sauce 1 tsp salt 1 tsp pepper After Saute: 2 tbsp butter 2 tbsp flour ½ cup beef broth Potato Mixture: 1 cup Water 1 ½ lbs russet potatoes peeled and cut into 1 inch cubes 2 tbsp butter 1 egg beaten 1 tsp kosher salt 1 tsp garlic powder To Finish: 1 cup shredded Cheddar cheese

Directions and total time – 30-60 m • Add ground beef and onion to the Instant Pot. Using the display panel select the SAUTE function. • Cook and stir until no pink remains. Drain any liquids. • Add remaining Beef Mixture ingredients and stir to combine. • In a small bowl, melt >2 tbsp butter. Whisk in flour and beef broth until smooth. Add to pot and stir to combine. • Cook and stir for 3-4 minutes, until sauce begins to thicken. •

Transfer the beef mixture to a 1 ½ qt Instant Pot-friendly casserole and cover to keep warm. • Rinse out the pot, then combine 1 cup water and cubed potatoes in the pot. • Turn the pot off by selecting CANCEL, then secure the lid, making sure the vent is closed. • Using the display panel select the MANUAL or PRESSURE COOK function. Use the +/- keys and program the Instant Pot for 8 minutes. • When the time is up, quick-release the pressure. • Add remaining Potato Mixture ingredients to the pot and mash to desired consistency. • Top the beef mixture evenly with the mashed potatoes. Cover the casserole with foil. • Rinse out the pot, then add 1 ½ cups of water and the steam rack. • Carefully lower the casserole onto the rack, then secure the lid, making sure the vent is closed. • Using the display panel select the MANUAL or PRESSURE COOK function. Use the +/- keys and program the Instant Pot for 10 minutes. • When the time is up, quick-release the pressure. • Carefully remove the dish from the pot, top with cheese and let rest for 10 minutes before serving. • (Optional) Set under broiler for 5-7 minutes until cheese is lightly browned.

Corned Beef with Cabbage

Ingredients for 6 servings:

3 carrots, peeled and cut into 3-inch pieces 1 yellow onion, peeled and quartered ½ pound small potatoes, halved 1 corned beef brisket (about 3 pounds), plus pickling spice packet or 1 tablespoon pickling spice 2 8-ounce beers 6 sprigs fresh thyme ½ head Savoy cabbage, cut into 1 ½-inch wedges ½ cup sour cream 3-4 tablespoons prepared horseradish, to taste

Directions and total time – more than 2 h To Cook in the Slow Cooker: • In a 5-to-6-quart slow cooker, place the carrots, onion and potatoes. Place corned beef, fat side up, on top of the vegetables and sprinkle with pickling spice. Pour the beers over the vegetables and brisket. Sprinkle with the sprigs of fresh thyme. Cover and cook on high until corned beef is tender, 5-6 hours or 10-12 hours on low. • Arrange cabbage over corned beef, cover, and continue cooking until cabbage is tender, 45 min to 1 hour (or 1 ½ to 2 hours on low). Thinly slice the corned beef against the grain and serve with the vegetables and cooking liquid with the horseradish sauce. To Cook in the Instant Pot: • Cut the corned beef into 2-3 chunks so it cooks faster and more evenly. Add to the insert of a 6 quart Instant Pot with the fat cap up. Layer with the onion, spices, thyme and beer. Cook on HIGH pressure for 90 minutes then do a quick release. • Add the potatoes, carrots and cabbage to the insert, close, and set to HIGH pressure for another 5 minutes. Natural release for 5 minutes, cut, and serve. For the Horseradish Sauce: • Mix the sour cream and horseradish together in a small bowl. Refrigerate for up to 1 week.

Beef and Barley Soup

Ingredients for 6-8 servings: 1 ½ pounds stew meat salt and pepper 2 tablespoons oil 10 baby bella mushrooms, quartered 3 cups mirepoix (just a combination of chopped onion, celery, and carrots) 6-8 cloves garlic, minced 6 cups low sodium beef broth (or vegetable) 1 cup water 2 bay leaves ½ teaspoon dried thyme 1 large potato, shredded (using a food processor or grater) ⅔ cup pearl barley, rinsed

Directions and total time – 1-2 h • Season the stew meat with a good pinch of salt and pepper. Heat 1 tablespoon of oil in a large pot or in the instant pot over medium-high heat. Add ½ the stew meat and brown on all sides for about 2-3 minutes total. Remove meat to a plate and repeat with the second batch and the second tablespoon of oil. • Add the mushroom to the pot and brown the mushrooms for 1-2 minutes or until they start picking up the brown bits left behind by the meat. Remove the mushrooms to the same plate as the stew meat. • If needed, add a little more oil to the pot and the mirepoix mix. Cook the veggies for 4-5 minutes or until the onions soften and become translucent. Add the garlic and cook for an additional 30 seconds ● Add the stew meat, mushrooms, bay leaves, dried thyme, water, and beef broth the to sautéed veggies in the instant pot, cover and pressure cook the meat for 13-16 minutes depending on the size of the stew meat. Allow the pressure to release before removing the lid.

Softly Turkey Breast

Ingredients for 6-8 servings: 7 lb bone-in turkey breast 3 tbsp butter softened ½ tsp paprika ¼ tsp garlic powder ½ tsp salt 1 ½ cups chicken broth or water 1 small onion quartered 2 small celery stalks cut in half 2 tbsp cornstarch Plus additional 1 tsp

Directions and total time – 30-60 m • If the turkey breast is frozen, let it thaw in refrigerator for 3 days in the wrapping it came in. Remove the gravy mix and giblets from the cavity, if any are present. Rinse the turkey breast and let it drain in a colander. Pat it dry with paper towels. Loosen the skin on top of the breast with your fingers and a knife but do not cut it off. • Combine butter, herb seasoning, and salt in a small bowl. Using fingertips, spread about 2 tbsp of the mixture up under the skin and onto the turkey breast. Lay the skin over the mixture then spread the remaining mixture on top of the skin. • Place the trivet in the Instant Pot pan and pour in the chicken broth. • If the turkey breast has a cavity to place the onion and celery under the breast, place it there. If it is open, just place them in the Instant Pot pan and place the turkey breast, breast side up. • Place lid on Instant Pot and set valve to "sealing". Press "Pressure Cook"/ "Manual" button, then -/+ button to 32 minutes on High Pressure. It will take about 12 to 20 minutes to come to pressure, cook 32 minutes, then when it beeps, let it release pressure naturally (don't touch sealing valve) for 20 minutes. If it hasn't release all the pressure, switch to "venting". Carefully open the lid away from your face when floating valve drops. • Preheat broiler. Remove the turkey with two large metal spatulas or spoons. Forks will release all the turkey juices! Place it on a foil-lined baking sheet and broil it 3 to 5 inches from the broiler for 3 to 5 minutes or just until skin in golden brown. • Measure 2 cups of turkey drippings in the Instant Pot pan. Discard any remaining liquid, onion and celery (I actually save them for soup later). Combine 1 tbsp water and cornstarch in a custard dish then pour into turkey drippings. Turn Instant Pot "Saute" button on. Cook the gravy, stirring constantly about 8 minutes or until slightly thickened.

Pork Meatball with Cream Sauce

Ingredients for 6 servings:

1 ¼ pounds ground pork 2 strips bacon minced 1 egg mixed ½ medium onion minced 2 tablespoons almond flour 1 clove garlic minced ¼ teaspoon pepper cracked ½ teaspoon sea salt 1 tablespoon tomato paste 1 tablespoon liquid aminos or tamari or soy sauce 2 tablespoons avocado oil or coconut oil 1 ½ cups Water or chicken stock 2 tablespoons butter salted, melted ½ teaspoon xanthan gum optional ⅔ cup heavy cream 33% ½ teaspoon sea salt ¼ teaspoon cracked pepper

Directions and total time – 30-60 m

• In a bowl mix the ground pork, bacon, egg, onion, almond flour, garlic, cracked pepper, sea salt and liquid aminos together. • Take 2 tablespoons of the meatball mixture and shape into a ball using wet hands. Place on a flat surface such as a cookie sheet. • Continue shaping meatballs. Makes about 24 weighing about 1 ounce each. • Press Sauté on the Instant Pot. Once display reads "hot", add avocado oil. • Carefully place half the meatballs into pot evenly spaced. After two minutes, turn them over. • After a minute, roll them onto a side. After another minute, remove and set aside on a plate. • Continue from step 5 to 7 with second batch of meat balls. • Once the second batch of meat balls are brown, remove and place with first batch. • Deglaze pot with water or chicken stock, be sure to scrape as much of the bits off the sides and bottom of the pan. • Add the meatballs back into the pot along with any drippings. Press cancel on the Instant Pot to stop Sauté. • Close lid and lock. Seal the pressure release valve. Press Manual and adjust to high pressure. Set time for 7 minutes to cook. • In the meantime, whisk xanthan gum into melted butter. • After cooking time is complete, press Cancel and Quick Release the pressure release valve. Unlock and open the lid. Remove the meatballs and set aside. • Press Sauté. Whisk in butter with xanthan gum into water/stock. • Next whisk in cream, salt and pepper in the Instant Pot. Let the sauce heat for 2 minutes while whisking. • Add the meatballs along with any drippings into the sauce and stir around to coat. • Ladle the meatballs with sauce into a bowl.

Chipotle Brisket

Ingredients for 4-6 servings:

3 ½ pounds beef brisket 1 tablespoons bacon fat 2 tablespoons chipotle powder 1 cup water 1 teaspoons fine sea salt ¼ cup chopped cilantro, for garnish1 tablespoon sesame oil

Directions and total time – 1-2 h

• Cut brisket into 4 equal pieces. • Add bacon fat to Instant Pot and turn to "saute." • Season brisket with chipotle powder by making sure it's applied liberally and rubbed into all sides. Once the fat is melted, add the beef to Instant Pot in two batches, searing brisket for 2-3 minutes per side until browned. Note: searing the beef all at once will cause overcrowding and will prevent the beef from browning nicely. • Once all beef is browned, add all pieces back to the pot along with water. • Close the instant pot, making sure the valve is set to "sealing" rather than "venting." Hit the "meat/stew" button and adjust to cook for 70 minutes. • Once the brisket is finished cooking, let the Instant pot release pressure naturally (about 15 minutes) until the lid easily opens. • Slice the beef against the grain and serve. Garnish with sea salt and cilantro, if desired.

Barbecue Spare Ribs

(Ready in about 35 minutes | Servings 8)

Per serving: 444 Calories; 33g Fat; 4.4g Carbs; 32.5g Protein; 1.7g Sugars

Ingredients

3 pounds spare ribs Sea salt and ground black pepper, to taste 1/2 teaspoon granulated garlic 1 teaspoon cayenne pepper For the sauce: 3/4 cup tomato puree A few drops of stevia 1 tablespoon balsamic vinegar 1/3 cup broth 1 cup water 1/3 teaspoon liquid smoke 1/2 teaspoon ground cloves

Directions

Season the ribs with salt, black pepper, garlic, and cayenne pepper. Add the spare ribs to the Instant Pot. Combine the ingredients for the sauce; whisk until everything is well mixed. Pour this sauce mixture over the spare ribs. Secure the lid. Choose the "Meat/Stew" setting and cook for 30 minutes under High pressure.

Once cooking is complete, use a natural pressure release; carefully remove the lid. You can thicken the cooking liquid with a tablespoon or two of flaxseed meal if desired. Enjoy!

Family Pork Roast

(Ready in about 30 minutes | Servings 6)

Per serving:

329 Calories;

18.2g Fat; 0g Carbs;

38.7g Protein;

0g Sugars

Ingredients

2 teaspoons peanut oil 2 pounds pork tenderloin 1 cup beef bone broth 2 bay leaves 1 teaspoon mixed peppercorns

Directions

Massage the peanut oil into the pork. Press the "Sauté" button to heat up the Instant Pot. Heat the oil and sear the meat for 2 to 3 minute on both sides. Add the broth, bay leaves and mixed peppercorns to the Instant Pot. Secure the lid. Choose the "Meat/Stew" setting and cook for 20 minutes under High pressure. Once cooking is complete, use a natural pressure release; carefully remove the lid. Serve over cauli rice. Bon appétit!

Lightning Source UK Ltd.
Milton Keynes UK
UKHW050948250521
384334UK00003B/249